Anxiety In Relationship

How to Overcome Anxiety, Insecurity and Negative Thinking.

Dealing with Jealousy and Attachment in Love.

Agnese Wolf

While most people are happy to put the past behind them, it is not so easy when you've been through a breakup. It may be one of the hardest things you will ever have to go through. People may tell you that time heals all wounds, but some wounds can take a long time to heal. But if you have the self confidence and determination that I have, then you can use these tips to heal from a breakup. You'll discover new strategies to deal with your feelings, how to move on with your life, and how to overcome that same old feeling of being heartbroken.

It is easier said than done, of course. But what's the alternative? Just holding on to it? Let time take its course? If this is the case, you must cease reading this material immediately. It's going to show you how to get over a breakup, not accept it!

Anxiety is such a crippling and undeserved mental health issue that is too often not talked about. It can take away your social life, your livelihood, and any sense of peace you have about yourself. It can make you feel frustrated and angry at the world around you because it seems so unfair. But there are so many ways to help ease it (despite how hard it feels right now) if only someone knew how to help. So, here's a brief intro on what this book will be about.

Whenever we think of anxiety in relationships, we automatically associate it with being uncomfortable or nervous around another person who might reject us or not be satisfied by our presence. We associate anxiety with almost everyone but our families because they're there for us no matter what. Overall, that's not a bad idea. Our families are people that we'll probably stick with through thick and thin, and there's no need to be anxious around them. But it is important to acknowledge this obvious fact—anxiety in romantic relationships is still very real and very much worth talking about.

The thing about romantic relationships is that it's two people coming together to spend time with each other, to make each other happy, and learn more about each other (and their likes/dislikes). If you feel anxious in the presence of your partner, then that's a huge red flag. Anxiety in a relationship is a bad sign because it means that you're not comfortable being close to them. It can't just be about being uncomfortable around your partner; it has to be more than that for them to worry about. If you avoid being close to your partner because of anxiety, then you need to go back and ask yourself "why?"

The most obvious reason why someone might react this way is if they have some sort of low self-esteem issues. If you have low self-esteem, then it can make interacting socially with others a challenge for you. And if your partner is making you feel this way, then it can make you avoid them. If this is an issue, then it's time to take a look at the root of it. You need to figure out why you have low self-esteem (and work on your issues with yourself) before getting into a relationship with someone else.

But there are other reasons why anxiety in relationships might surface. There's an even more common one that happens often—it's known as codependency. If two people are codependent towards each other, meaning they're both dependent on each other for their happiness, then this can be especially damaging for one or both parties involved in the relationship. If you feel like you need your partner for your happiness, then you probably won't be able to function well in the relationship. You'll also probably make the partner feel like they're responsible for your happiness, which isn't fair to them. You can be with someone and not feel like they're responsible for your happiness, but if you can't handle it yourself, then it's time to reconsider whether or not this relationship is worth it.

Another reason why anxiety in relationships happens is because of how it's presented in media (specifically romantic media). It's a media craze that romantic relationships are a cure for mental health problems when in reality, that couldn't be further from the truth. If you're anxious around your partner, then that's a sign that your mental health isn't where it should be. That doesn't mean that you're going to stay this way, it means you need to admit to yourself and your partner that you have some work to do with yourself before making any other decisions about the relationship.

Anxiety in relationships can come from so many different sources—and there's no shame in admitting it when it gets to you. You can talk to your partner about it, or you can try reaching out to a mental health professional. What's important is that you don't feel uncomfortable being around the person you love, because it means there are some cracks somewhere in the relationship. And if those cracks don't get fixed, then the relationship won't last long.

Dating and Anxiety

If you are dating someone with relationship anxiety or involved in a relationship with this person, then you probably already understand how destructive these feelings can be. You might often feel like the anxiety is the third person in your relationship; the third wheel that makes a couple being just a little more complicated. This third person will get between you and your partner and sow confusion and doubt at every turn. You can't tell your heart where to love, and you certainly didn't enter this relationship with the idea that anxiety was going to fill your days with difficulties. Anxiety does not need to ruin your relationship. It does not need to put such a strain on your relationship that you are not able to enjoy being a couple or even to make you think about calling it quits. If you understand how anxiety works and how it is affecting your relationship, you will be better prepared to overcome the effects of anxiety when it does enter your relationship. Overcoming the anxiety can push the two of you deeper into your relationship, making it stronger and more fulfilling than it was before. There are things that you need to be willing to accept and the concept of relationship anxiety if you are going to be able to help your partner and sustain your relationship:

- Anxiety is real and exists in your relationship. This is not something that your partner made up, and it is not something that you are imagining. It exists. Anxiety is normal, and it is only a problem if it threatens to overwhelm the relationship.

- The effects of relationship anxiety can prevent the two of you from enjoying the deep, meaningful relationship you were meant to enjoy.

- Anxiety is not necessarily life-threatening, but it can make your life miserable by dealing with it.

- No one wants to experience relationship anxiety. People who have this anxiety don't want it, and they don't want you to suffer from their problems.

- The symptoms of the anxieties can subside for long periods and then recur at odd moments. They may attack for weeks and months or only pop up occasionally.

- There is nothing rational or logical about anxiety. People who have anxieties will fear things that don't exist and have doubts about things that may never happen. They will act irrationally at times. It will do no good to tell your partner not to worry because this will probably make them worry more.

- Anxiety does not mean that you or your partner is weak. On the contrary, living with anxieties and trying to hold together some semblance of normality indicates that you are stronger than you think you are. It is not easy trying to live a good life when the people who were supposed to help you as a child failed you and gave you all of these anxieties.

You need to be aware that a person who has anxieties does not look at the relationship in the same way that you do. They will always be seeing things in a different light, imagining that things are different from the way that you see them. Your partner is probably spending a good part of their time worrying about the relationship and thinking of all the things that could be going wrong and probably already are. Here are some of the things that your partner may be dwelling on:

- I always reach out first with needs.
- I text my partner, but my partner doesn't always text back immediately.
- Most of the people out there are better than me.
- Another person could give my partner more than I do.
- My partner is hiding something from me.
- My partner is probably lying about how much they love me.
- I know my partner thinks about cheating on me.
- I feel my lover does not share the same level of love that I have for them.
- I feel anxious all of the time.

Having a few of these thoughts sometimes is normal; having many of them all the time is not normal. When anxiety becomes part of your relationship, then your partner is probably thinking these thoughts all the time. Their mind is creating disastrous scenarios where the relationship goes sour, and they are left alone again. Sometimes their anxieties will make them act in ways that are guaranteed to annoy you or even push you away. As an example, imagine that your partner is full of anxiety over the communication in your relationship. Your partner may feel that they are always the ones to reach out to first. They may question the length of time that it takes you to respond to their phone texts or calls. They might feel that you would not even speak to them if they did not contact you first. So, they begin to pull away and stop contacting you. This strategy will force you to be the one to make the first contact if you really want to talk to them. They may not answer immediately the first few times. They may be a test for you to see if you will continue to contact them even if you don't receive an answer in return. When they begin to feel better about the depth of your commitment, then they might become a bit more communicative. Knowing that you will contact them first makes them feel that they are worth the effort that you are making. Their test was successful because you are still there. You have proven that their irrational fear that you are not as committed as they are is untrue. And this may only last for a little while before they feel the need to test you again.

Thinking that anxiety has the power to ruin a relationship might seem a bit dramatic, but it very well can. Anxiety is an overpowering emotion that can cripple a relationship. When anxiety intrudes on one or both of the partners in a relationship, it will eventually encroach on the relationship itself. Anxiety will affect your actions, emotions, and thoughts. It will lead to misinterpretations and cloud your perceptions and your judgment. Anxiety will drag you down into a pit of misery. When these things happen to one or both of the partners in a relationship, it has the power to cause them a considerable amount of misunderstanding and stress. The relationship can be totally destroyed when anxiety is allowed to cause worries, make you wonder "what if?" or taints your behaviors, thoughts, and emotions. These things will ultimately push out anything positive that once existed between the two partners. When someone is living with anxiety, their life can become increasingly restricted as those anxious and negative beliefs and thoughts become the most significant things in their lives. More relationship issues are experienced by people who have generalized anxiety. People who suffer from anxiety are more likely to have issues and problems in their relationships than people who don't regularly experience anxiety.

When anxiety intrudes into a relationship, the entire situation can become extremely stressful. Both the person who suffers from anxiety and their partner can suffer from the adverse effects of this. The central theme in the relationship becomes stress. Greater distance comes between the partners as they begin to feel the barriers that the anxiety causes them to erect. This is an unhealthy situation that can easily lead to the death of the relationship. The reason why anxiety has the power to ruin relationships is that it intrudes upon them.

Anxiety not only causes people to have negative beliefs and patterns of thought, but it can also make those anxiety-ridden thoughts become more massive than they really are. The issues that are created by anxiety will erode the ability of the two partners to trust each other and their feelings of being connected to each other. The person who suffers from anxiety and their partner will both spend too much time giving attention to anxiety itself and not to the relationship. This misdirected attention will lead to feelings of abandonment, separation, and disconnection from each other. If anxiety had its own voice, it would use that voice to shout mean things at the partner of the person who is suffering from the anxiety and at the person who is suffering the anxiety. That is what anxiety does. It speaks with words of self doubt that will ultimately erode any rational thought either partner might have, and it will twist their words into something unfriendly. The beliefs and thoughts of the partner who has anxiety will cause them to feel negative emotions like:

- You are a bad partner.
- Your partner is planning on leaving you.
- You are not competent.
- You need to protect your partner.
- You do not deserve the love of your partner.

Breaking Up — Get over the Initial Pain

There is much more to a bad relationship or marriage than a few disagreements. Have you ever heard about frogs and boiling water?
No?

A frog, if placed in boiling water, will jump straight out, however, alternatively if a frog is placed in cold water, and the water is set to boil, the frog won't register the slow increase in temperature and will ultimately boil to death. Sound disturbing?

Well, believe it or not, that is exactly what a bad relationship is. A bad relationship often consists of major issues, if you had known about them before, or immediately after the relationship began; you would have walked away without batting an eye. But that's not what happened — instead, what happened was that further along, you started noticing little things, things that you didn't want to make a big fuss about because it was just one thing. And then that thing became a daily thing, and there were 10 other things, but by then you were so far in, you couldn't even imagine what it would be like to walk away. You had begun to lose your identity to your 'couple' identity.

The result is you, walking through a day with your head down, afraid to be told by the person, who is supposed to be your other half, that you aren't good enough, or that you are being paranoid, and that your paranoia is destroying what you've built together. It is about your significant other appearing oblivious, as you feel like you are sinking in this pit of hopelessness, and no matter how loud you scream, no one can hear you, except one person — and that person does not seem to care.

A large part of this issue is triggered by moving too fast in a relationship. Many relationships initially seem to be going great, because you are caught up in the whirlwind, and as a result, you don't recognize the real-life problems until it's too late. For other relationships, the trigger is the sense of unrealistic expectations or over-dependency. And if none of those are, there are always the classic issues of dishonesty, deception, emotional baggage, and even sex issues, all of which we will be discussing, but first, let's address the issue of a 'couple identity' so that we can have a clearer understanding going forward.

What Is Meant by Couple Identity?
A common rookie mistake in many relationships is made by people who allow their likes and dislikes as a couple to influence and, in a moment, takeover their likes and dislikes as

an individual. Initially, this is usually a method of small scale self-sacrifice, like making sure you always give him or her control of the remote, or the last bite of pie, but gradually these little things add up, and at one point you find yourself thinking about what he/she wants, as opposed to what you want — the problem is that 'we' is not all about 'them', it's about both of you, and by trying to prioritize them, you are losing sight of yourself, and while you may think this isn't a big deal, and that you can live without having certain things, continuously delegating yourself to bottom of the food-chain, creates a sort of resentment, that later subconsciously manifests in your behavior.

To start with — 'Whirlwind Relationships' — as romantic as they may sound, are inherently one of the riskiest relationship types. Not only do you go into a relationship too fast to identify and adjust to your partner's personality, but you also go into the relationship falling for all the best sides of your significant other, without really accounting for the cons that balance them out, and how equipped you are to deal with them. As a result, the further along you get into the relationship, the further apart you seem to get. The 'Couple Complex' only makes this even harder to deal with, because, on the one hand, you keep seeing glimpses of the person you want to be in a relationship with, but on the other hand, the continuous bombardment of 'disagreements' is exhausting and start taking its toll on the both of you.

There is the 'Fairytale Fallout'

Boy meets girl — girl meets boy — He thinks she is a Goddess, and literally can't do 'anything wrong' — She thinks he is Rhett Butler and Prince Charming rolled into one perfect package, who exists for the sole purpose of making her feel loved, and cherished, as well as everything in between.

Sounds Pretty Perfect Doesn't It?

The only problem is — real life isn't perfect. It's messy and complicated and at a time when the hot mess that is life hits you, you are going to be left reeling from the impact. That is why in healthy relationships; you acknowledge both the pros and cons of your partner, which in turn allows them to do the same for you. Not only does this help minimize unrealistic expectations, but it also helps ground your relationship. For this reason, the reality's absence, in the form of rose-colored glasses, when you have 'couple identity' issues, basically turns fairytale romances into nightmares.

Finally, let's come to the worst possible way "couple identity" can adversely influence a relationship — dependency. Now to be clear, there is nothing wrong with being dependent on somebody, especially when you are sharing your life with someone. There is, however, a very big problem when dependence becomes 'overdependence'.

As sweet as it may sound, 'depending' on your partner, is the stepping stone of identity crisis — who are you without them — who are they without you? You need to remember — you fell in love with an actual person — not the shadow of someone who needs you to supplicate his/her every decision.

What's worse, dependency is never just about needing validation from your significant other — it may start like that, but soon enough you start questioning why they aren't looking for that same validation from you — and then you start wondering if they are getting that validation from somewhere else because if they are, then every friend they have is suddenly someone you are suspicious of, and as a result, resent. It doesn't sound so lovey-dovey anymore now, does it?

Another thing you may want to ask yourself is why you are in the relationship. While it's easy enough to say it's because you are in love with your partner, love isn't some magical potion that just drops itself on you — that is attraction. Love grows, which means there has to be a seed, and sometimes, like it or not, the seeds are far from positive — sometimes relationships start based on fear, or worse, change expectations. Any of these, or any other similar reasons, can and will mean, your relationship is based on nothing more than a lie.

Speaking of Lies, Let's Talk About Lies

Occasionally, there are relationship issues that are so explicitly 'breakup triggers', that it is impossible to understand why anyone would even contemplate continuing a relationship under those circumstances — yet somehow, you are still there.

Dishonesty Is Possibly at the Top of this List

Dishonesty is often seemingly innocent, like a white lie, to come off as a cooler person, or a more desirable partner. But what you need to acknowledge is that if your partner is comfortably lying to you about little insignificant things — this means that first, he/she doesn't seem to care much about breaking your trust in them if they are willing to break it over something so minor, and on second, if he/she is lying to you about the little things, what guarantee do you have that they aren't lying to you about the big things?

You don't. And the truth is that 9 out of 10 times, both tidbits apply — meaning, if your significant other is lying to you, chances are you are being lied about more than you think, but you probably already know that, don't you?

But while on the one hand there is deception, on the other hand, there is the equally burdensome issue of emotional baggage. Let's face facts, if you aren't in high school, chances are you aren't going to be someone's first relationship, even if you are, there is usually a story, a reason why, and that particular story isn't very pretty.

The existence of a past isn't a massive issue — that would be ridiculous. What can take a toll on a relationship, however, is history that isn't history — an ex-girlfriend or boyfriend who cheated, or was abusive, who your partner sees in you every time you walk a certain way or talk a certain way. The truth is, not everyone is capable of dealing with someone who has emotional baggage, and pretending that you are, is simply more damaging than just bravely acknowledging your shortcomings, and allowing them to move on. Remember, a relationship is not just about what is good for you — it is about what is good for both parties.

The final possible issue — and the one nobody, for some unfortunate reason, wants to acknowledge, is sexual compatibility. Sexuality is an important part of intimate relationships and one that most people, even long-term partners, find difficult to discuss, which is why one of the most debilitating factors of modern-day relationships, is lack of sexual equality or lack of open sexual conversation.

The reason this factor is considered so taboo — is because it can be difficult to tell a partner that they aren't physically satisfying you, or to even have to acknowledge that you aren't satisfying them. Yes, couples' therapy is an option, and you can try to work it out, but despite everything, there are times when it's just not enough.

The Quick-Start Guide to Recovering Fast — What Not to Do

A depressed person needs the support of the people around them, particularly those with whom they have close relationships. This can be difficult in depressive illness. As unhappy individuals may withdraw from social activities, express a lack of interest in participating in formerly pleasurable activities, and may build a wall with their significant others that renders communication with them difficult.

At this point, these issues faced by depressed individuals and their loved ones are nothing new. The first step is naturally to have the right approach to your partner's condition. This is a condition that they are dealing with and if you want to help them, you may have to occasionally put some of your personal feelings and needs to the side, at least briefly.

Being on the side of your feelings and desires can be very difficult for some people. Let's face it. We live in a narcissistic age. Men and women who watch self-help videos or read inspirational books may be familiar with this idea that if someone is a source of negative energy in your life, then you should consider cutting them out. This may appear to be a natural thing to do, but it isn't, though it is important to note that this type of thinking is very characteristic of the modern world.

Many families may have had an uncle or parent with a substance abuse problem or someone else who was dealing with a bad marriage or joblessness. Is the solution to simply cut that person out of your life? Although many people today may see this as something viable and even ideal, it is clear that the institution of the family has been somewhat eroded by the difficulty that modern people seem to have in acting in a truly selfless manner.

Yes, a depressed person may be frustrating to deal with because of their moods and the "wall" they build, but people like this need family more than others. It is not beneficial to these people (or to their families) for them to be cut off because of their dysfunction. Some of the most talented people in human history suffered from melancholia or depression and you may be tossing a talented person who may one day be beneficial to you and others to the side by perceiving their illness as something inconvenient for you.

So, the point here is that a little altruism goes a long way. By being a little selfless in trying to help your significant other who is depressed, you may find that one day someone may behave selflessly towards you in your time of trouble. That may be a spouse helping you through your depressive illness or someone else helping you through another problem.

Alright, with that long warning on the side, we can start talking about how a spouse can support a significant other who is depressed. Some of these proposals are straightforward, while others are more nuanced and may require some thought to fully comprehend.

Tip 1. Do Not Be Judgmental

This first tip may be a no-brainer for some readers. That said, it is not a nobrainer so it is important to mention it here. Depression is difficult to deal with for everyone, including the depressed individual. One of the reasons why there is so much stigma surrounding depression is that many people have preconceived notions about it. These notions may come from perceptions they have about unhappy people they have seen or from misconceptions about why a particular person is depressed.

"Snap out of it" is something that someone may be inclined to say to a depressed person. In the past, a statement like this might have been perfectly reasonable to say to someone who is depressed but now we understand that depression stems ultimately from disorders in brain chemistry so the individual may not be able to snap out of it. Perhaps, the first effective step that you can take towards supporting someone who is depressed is by deciding not to be judgmental. Depressive illness is hard. This condition looks different in different people and does not go away when we project our negative judgments onto depressed people.

Tip 2. Educate Yourself About Depression First, Before You Plan Your "Strike"

In reality, you the reader have taken one of the most significant first steps in supporting someone with sadness. Men and women are often judgmental when it comes to depressed people because they do not know much about depression. A person who has never experienced depression is sure to have a host of preconceived notions that impact how they perceive depressed people that they meet, even when that person is a close family member, such as a spouse or a child partner.

Therefore, before you even begin to think about a "plan of attack" in dealing with sadness in a significant other you need to first make sure that you have an understanding of depression. You should understand what depression is, what some of the causes of depression are, what the warning signs are, and how sadness can drastically impact the lives of depressed people and those around them. If you didn't want to read this book, you wouldn't have some interest in educating yourself on the subject so let the education continue.

Tip 3. Avoid the Confrontational and Interventional Approach

It is easy to see depression as something dysfunctional in another person's life that simply needs to go away. There are television shows that involve handling dysfunction from what can be thought of as an intervention or interventional approach. What does this signify in terms of depression is pouncing or cornering the depressed person (often with other family and loved ones involved) to impress the person on how damaging their condition has been to themselves and the people around them.

Although this sort of approach may be effective in people with substance abuse disorders, it is probably not the best approach for dealing with sadness in a relationship. Your significant other should be someone that you trust and who trusts you. They most likely are looking to you as someone that they can go to for support, and they may be waiting for the opportunity to broach the subject of depression with you if they have not already. Confronting them angrily or forcefully with their depression is not necessary and is potentially harmful. There are various options for dealing with this problem, some of which you will learn more about below.

Tip 4. Use Gimple Gestures to Show that You care

Although some readers may approach this book as a weapon in their arsenal to declare war on depression and winning it, in reality, a depressed person may simply need to know that you care. Although the war analogy may be apt for the depression subject when it comes to supporting someone who is depressed, it might be better to think about depression as an illness. Someone who is suffering from an illness does not want to be attacked or confronted.

Sure, you may feel that as you are not depressed you are perfectly poised to help your unhappy partner, but you have to recognize that they are doing things they have the authority to do so independently time. As much as you may want this sadness to go away now, the person may need some time to cope with their depression and formulate a way of dealing with it. In this regard, depression can be like a grieving process. It is something that people go through and what they may need during this time is a kind word, a card, or some gesture that indicates that you care.

Tip 5. Do Not Project Your Perceptions and Experiences onto the Other Person

Depression is a subjective experience. One of the amazing aspects of it is this. Even though we can say that depressive illness results from a chemical imbalance that is probably related to concentrations of serotonin, norepinephrine, dopamine, and other neurotransmitters at synapses in certain parts of the brain, we still have to recognize that each depressed person is an exceptional individual with their unique set of thoughts and experiences.

That means that, even if you educate yourself about depression, you will be unable to access certain components of your significant other's subjective experience of depression. Just as you have aspects of yourself that other people do not understand, also your partner has aspects of him/herself that you do not comprehend. This tip is related to the advice not to judge, although it is not the same. as a loving partner, you must be careful not to project your perceptions of depression and why they may be depressed onto your partner. The goal here is not to be Dr. Freud, but to be an effective supporter.

Tip 6. Stay Away from Tough-Love Approaches to Handling Depression

Just as a confrontational intervention is often ineffective in supporting a depressed person, so is the tough love approach. In the context of depression in a relationship, this approach may consist of forcibly dragging your loved one out of bed, forbidding them from engaging in some behaviors associated with their depression, or giving them an ultimatum of some sort, such as saying that you will leave if they do not get help.

Although many people reach their breaking points when it comes to dealing with the illnesses of those they love, the goal is to steer your partner in the right direction and do that supportively. You do not want to push your partner away by being harsh when they needed you to be kind. We remember how others treat us when we are down and the last thing you want your partner to do is to think about you like the most uncaring person that they had to deal with in their trial period.

Tip 7. Stay Away from Comparisons with Yourself or Others Who Have Also Experienced a Depressive Illness

There is a lot of baggage surrounding depression. This condition is common. So many people think they understand it. Some individuals have experienced being down because of a traumatic or sad event in their life and they may conclude that this is just what depressive illness is — a brief period that weak people experience when something bad happens.

As you, the reader, have gleaned as you have read this far, depression is a serious condition that can be linked to chemical imbalances in the brain. It runs in families and even some severe medical states like brain cancer can cause depression. Just because you experience being sad when your gerbil died does not give you a perch from which to compare what your partner is experiencing to you.

The best thing to do in those situations is to engage with your partner consistently. How do you interact with your partner? What is your form of communication? You can talk about issues repeatedly, but it's difficult to fix unresolved problems if you do not lower yourself to the level of your partner when communicating. The good news is that you will work with your partner to overcome romantic vulnerability. It requires time, efficient communication, and the ability to strengthen your relationship.

Here's how to cope with emotional insecurities:

Meet Each Other's Needs

- Every single person in the world has several basic needs.
- We all are committed to making sure that we can escape pain and suffering.
- We want diversity in life.
- We want to feel important.

Therefore, connection to others is crucial. All needs are in the hierarchy of how important they are. You need to know the most important need of your spouse. Does your relationship help fulfill your emotional needs? If not, how can you change the way your partner is treated and appreciated?

Balance the Polarity

In every normal relationship, there is always one male and one female energy. Such energy sources must not be gender-related but opposing powers must be present to achieve romantic peace.

This definition is referred to as polarity. Have you built an unequaled relationship with your partner? It may cause anxiety when both partners take on masculine or feminine traits. These positions have changed over time. How can polarity be restored and insecurity banned from a relationship?

Cherish Each Other Like a New Couple

New couples want to meet and actively approach each other whenever they can. This initial desire disappears with time. Once you get to know your partner better, both of you seem not to treasure and adore each other as much. The routine of daily life makes you relax and cease to please your spouse.

Insecurities will start to show when your partner feels your attraction for them has vanished. During this time, it's important to restore your love and behave like you did when you started to date. Love your spouse more than your friends. Appreciate your spouse by complimenting and scheduling incredible dates. Be thoughtful and write them love notes. This little behavior can lead to diminish anxiety and make your partner feel desired.

Create New Memories

Mistakes are bound to occur in any relationship, but both of you must make sure they do not stay. Also, if you have struggled over financial affairs before, it is time to put those old problems behind in case you want to go forward as a couple.

Seek to change your attitude rather than demand that your partner stops doing what disturbs you. Support your partner and resolve together to create a lovely new story rather than to relieve the pain of the past.

Occasional insecurity exists in the most stable relationships. You cannot control your partner's feelings, but you should do your best to support them.

What Do I Do If This Kills My Vulnerability?

Jealousy at first is cute, but it can lead to a poisonous wedge between partners. Many of us experience self-doubt, which is natural, every now and then. Yet it can potentially lead to a wedge between you and your partner when it comes to jealousy over communications, personal insecurity, and contrast.

In some ways, vulnerability is good because it makes your relationship intimate and increases your partner's worth. But, if there is too much fear, it can create a toxic environment and damage your confidence. Insecurity can also separate partners who love one another and care for each other.

When doubt or jealousness first comes to light, it always seems innocent and a little cute. However, it can cause you to act out of control in a relationship that seems to be going on smoothly. To improve your relationship, you and your partner should establish resolutions. Here are some examples that you and your partner should focus on.

Self-Esteem

Self-esteem is difficult to remove, but in it lies your negative mentality, which makes it difficult to eliminate. Improving your self-esteem is the best way to get rid of (or at least diminish) your insecurities. How can you do that? Encourage yourself by booking a relaxing spa day, start to work out, or doing something you want. The best thing is to focus on a problem you want to get rid of and build on it.

Find Out the Root Cause

You cannot dismiss any obstacle until you accept that it exists. Dig deep and think back about your existing relationship to know what is causing you so much grief. Was there anything your mother said that was stuck with you as far back as age five? Is your partner doing something that challenges your motivation? Either way, if you know the source of your fear, then you are ready to take on it.

Trust Yourself and Your Partner

No one will be surprised to admit confidence as the main factor for happy and healthy relations. The term "trust" does only mean sharing your deepest secrets with your spouse. It is also necessary to have faith in your instincts. If you've never had a reason to distrust your spouse, don't!!! Nonetheless, if you sense that something is not right in your mind, trust your instincts!

Stop Overthinking

Do not consider it a personal problem when your partner decides they want to hang out with their friends one evening without you. Not all that your partner does in any way is supposed to harm you. If your partner sleeps before does not mean they are cheating—it just means that they are tired.

You Both Need Space to Breathe and Have a Healthy Relationship

It will help to keep your partner from feeling smothered or targeted. You should also follow your interests and strive to preserve your own social life. Doing things by yourself will improve your confidence. Note that beyond your romantic relationships, you still have your own life to live.

Let Go of the Negative Past

Prior encounters will screw up your love life. You should stop recalling how a mysterious ex made you feel before they bring insecurities into your new relationship. Only if you let go of your bad memories will you move forward.

Speak with a therapist, friends, family, or your current spouse about your past encounters, "sometimes it's just cathartic to let it all go." Speaking honestly about hurtful experiences in the past will help your new partner better understand you. And let's face it, it's just cathartic to let it go sometimes.

Don't Stop Conversation

Talking is a significant aspect of interaction and in relationships is among the most common dating advice that you will often see.

Be Careful

Be careful of your time on social media, many distractions are rampant on social media nowadays. Some women flaunt their nakedness all over the social, and this can make you compare their body shape with the shape of your spouse, making you feel the shape of your spouse is horrible. Everybody on social media only posts the best pictures and best moments.

Not to mention, if you're inclined to harass your partner's exes on social media it will not help you to overcome your insecurities.

Discuss

Discuss with true friends how you feel. No one wants to be alone, why should you talk to a group of good friends about your feelings? If you've got a group of amazing friends, bring together your most trusted friends and share your innermost feelings and thoughts.

Not only does discussing your problems ease some of the fears you have but also your friends can share their personal experiences in resolving confusion or envy matters.

Channel

Channel your anxieties into something positive. If you want to dismiss petty jealousy in relationships, start to exercise or do anything constructive where possible. This may sound crazy, but it will motivate you to improve your selfesteem and foster good mental health for at least 30 minutes a day. Research indicates that daily exercise can help to decrease anxiety, depression, and mood.

The key to dealing with anxiety and finding the love you deserve is truly inside of you! What happened in the past is in the past, also you can rewire your brain to concentrate on your positive attributes and to silence that negative script constantly running in your head.

You might want to enlist the assistance of a trusted friend, partner or therapist, to help you look at these thoughts as objectively as possible, find out what makes you angry and how to deal with it, stop for a second and reevaluate before responding, how to calm yourself and learn a new positive, secure attachment style.

There are many habits you can learn to help you achieve this.

Slay those Dragons, Find Love and Contentment

You do not have to be a victim of your past.

Building up security in relationships by developing a safe connection with a friend, psychotherapist, or working with your securely attached romantic partner, is the best way to light that fire inside of you and nurture it until this can flourish on its own, in a secure and emotionally mature adult romantic relationship.

The most crucial part of this adventure is to reconcile with your childhood experiences, understand how the unconscious decisions helped you survive, impacted your behaviors, and comprehend how your past relationships impact your present relationships also will continue to do so in the future unless changes are made.

Patience

The struggle is real and very human. Patience is a virtue and refers to our ability to tolerate provocation without responding in anger or annoyance, to persevere in the face of delay or forbearance when faced with stress or strain in the longer term.

Patience is a critical coping skill and an invaluable skill to learn; it is a way to find emotional freedom and a lifelong spiritual practice.

Patience is not about being passive or resigned to your fate, but about taking control of your emotions, finding your power, and knowing when to respond or act.

It is simple in today's world to become frustrated when things do not happen when you want them to, and easy to lose you're cool over something that is not justified in generating so much frustration and emotion.

Understanding

The anxiously attached person's persistent uneasiness, frustrations, neediness, anxieties, and worries will eventually permeate into the relationship, no matter how secure your spouse is.

Because they are more inclined to choose dismissive or avoidant partners, the interpersonal interactions are complicated further.

You must learn to see the impact of your insecure behaviors on your partner and others with whom you engage.

Positive Self-Talk and Prayer

Sometimes your negative self-talk just runs rampant. You ruminate and think the same negative thoughts over and over again.

It is possible, though, to create new thought processes and replace the wellworn paths of negativity. This can be extremely powerful.

It is not about turning off negative thoughts or trying to improve your mood by turning it into a positive version; it is about objectively framing the negative thought if it is true. This way, you can find a way to move forward.

When you are triggered by events to spiral into negative thoughts, you can also find other coping mechanisms to calm yourself down.

Some people find great comfort in prayer. Closing your eyes, or casting them to the heavens or mountains, and talking your troubles through with your maker, can be very calming and is a good coping mechanism to center yourself and finding courage.

People think meditation is about clearing your head. Mindfulness is about being in the present moment, experiencing what you are experiencing; in other words, this is it. Be fully present.

Mindfulness means bringing non-judgmental awareness to the present moment and has been shown in many studies to help focus attention, diminish pain, and help calm yourself.

Sleep

The quality and quantity of food affect every system in the body quantity of sleep you get, especially the brain. Your mental health requires that reset button that allows your body to heal, rest and recuperate.

It may be a bit of a catch 22 situation, as anxiety is often the cause for insomnia, and lack of sleep makes your anxiety worse, so you must learn how to allow yourself to relax and get the required hours of uninterrupted sleep.

Sleep gives your neurons a chance to shut down and do the necessary repairs, without which they start to malfunction. Sleep provides the proteins needed for this repair and is integral to healthy emotional and social functioning.

One of the most significant purposes of sleep is that it allows you to relax to help us solidify and consolidate memories, thus helping us to retain information and newly learned skills.

Consistent, good-quality sleep plays a major role in the brain's connectivity and plasticity (learning and memory).

Sleep deprivation has been likened to driving under the influence — it affects every function in your body and can mess up your ability to think clearly, be objective, make informed decisions, and communicate appropriately. It inhibits your ability to choose what to pay attention to and regulate your emotions.

Workout

Physical health benefits include heart health, reduced inflammation, increased bone density, muscle strength, increased metabolism, and burning calories major spikes in your immune system. It reduces the risk of metabolic syndrome, arthritis, depression, and anxiety.

Whether it is an individual achievement or a team achievement, the pride that follows acts as a major confidence booster, as well as a mood lifter. Team sports help to build relationships and social networks, which are crucial for dealing with stress and becoming more resilient.

Stop Competing with Your Partner

Present your authentic self to all your relationships in the firm belief that you are enough. If you feel that you are not enough and have to prove yourself to others and your partner, you will engage in a dangerous competing game with your spouse.

It may start with something simple, like who is right or wrong about an irrelevant statement, or who lost a board game, but it may soon morph into a fierce competition about who is more popular or good looking, whose job is more important, or who is the better parent.

Your spouse is not the enemy. You both have to commit yourself to be the best you can be in the relationship, the family you are making together, or the life you are building together, but you have to be your authentic self and feel safe enough to make mistakes and be supported.

Perhaps, you raise your voice to make a point, and soon you are both shouting; maybe you retreat to another room or ignore your partner until they apologize. Once a relationship becomes a battlefield, it is no longer a safe relationship, nor is it fun.

It is always better to be present than to be right. If you are in any discussion to win, you enter a slippery slope of turning your relationship into a battlefield.

It's natural to argue and fight but beware of changing from being on the same team to being an adversary. When your fights start to feel like playing a game of sport, step back and re-evaluate.

Another clear sign of competing is not being honest with your partner, for whatever reason. Presenting anything other than your true self is disrespectful and puts you in competition with yourself and your partner. This prohibits vulnerability, as well as honest communication.

If you cannot be genuinely happy for your partner's success, you start feeling resentment and will soon find it difficult to spend time in their presence. You need to communicate your feelings and why it bothers you.

Trying to make each other jealous is an extremely destructive way of getting attention. Using it to make your partner jealous is toxic also destructive because it is a sign of competition and trying to belittle them. Stirring up a little competition to keep things fresh is manipulative and dishonest.

Belittling comments may come across as silly little jibes, but it is demoralizing, and done to hurt is critical and disrespectful. If you disguise it as a joke, it makes it even worse because you are not honest enough to voice your feelings or needs, you want to cut your partner down, as well as make them feel small, and then get away by claiming it was a joke that makes them feel even smaller.

If you or your partner is not able to compromise, it is a really bad sign that you compete. Wanting everything done your way is not being respectful or caring towards your partner.

Throwing out ultimatums typically follows the 'unable to compromise phase,' threatening to leave or stating that if your lover genuinely cared about you, they would do what you want, and this is both a form of mental and emotional abuse. You are testing each other and getting sucked into the unhealthiest doldrums of any relationship. Unless you get help to understand the underlying insecurities, as well as lack of respect, you have little chance of saving the relationship.

Keeping It Going

Rather than competing with your partner to get validation, spend your energy on keeping your love.

One of the most effective ways to keep track of things is to have a journal the spark alive is a novelty. Doing new, exciting, and challenging activities together have huge benefits for relationships. When you first started dating, you 'took on' each other's interests and expanded your life.

Finding new ways to do different and exciting things instead of getting bored and looking for excitement outside the relationship can broaden your horizons and put a fresh spin on your relationship.

Rekindling the early stages of the relationship, maintaining novelty, and suspension of judgment is critical to keeping a relationship from becoming a battlefield.

Fun Activities

There are lots of ways to find healthy and exciting habits to enhance romantic interest and wake up your sexual appetite.

Engaging in fun and physically arousing experiences can broaden your world to exciting adventures with someone you feel emotionally safe with, without resorting to fanning the fear of rejection to keep the passion alive.

You can think about your own; some examples include:

- Watching emotionally charged movies, such as action, comedy, or romance
- Cycling
- Hiking
- Playing tennis or racquetball
- Brisk walks
- Game night at the local pub on the same team
- Dancing
- Traveling to places you have not visited yet

No one wants to feel insecure. And any jealousy that we get is an implicit feeling. The problem of jealousy is not the stage; it rarely pops up, but it occurs even though we do not get hold of it. When we encourage our envy to overtake us or change the tense way, we feel about ourselves and our general surroundings, we see what happens. That's why understanding where our jealous feelings come from and find out how to respond to jealousy in a positive, successful way, from our close ties with our company to our own goals, is crucial to so many facets of our lives.

What Is Jealousy?

Jealousy is a series of feelings accompanied by anger and unhappiness because someone or something you desire belongs to someone else. Wikipedia defines it as feelings and thoughts of fear, concern, and insecurity due to a lack of something.

Jealousy can manifest as more than one emotion; resentment, disgust, anger, bitterness, helplessness, inadequacy, suspicion, hostility, and desperation. It is the fear that you may lose something or someone you consider indispensable to someone else.

It is feeling angry and down in the dumps because someone you love is interested in someone else and maybe is paying attention to them, and sometimes another person is showing interest in them. Also, because someone has something you wish you had.

So, Why Are We So Jealous?

Studies have shown predictably that elevated aggression coincides with reduced self-esteem. "Many of us often neglect the intrinsic shame that exists within us because it is easy to speak about ourselves with self-critical thoughts. Furthermore, the degree to which we feel insecure and anxious may be deeply influenced by the remorse of our experience," said Dr. Lisa Firestone, author of Addressing the Critical Internal Voice. As Dr. Robert Firestone and her father pointed out, "strong inner voice" is a form of destructive self-talk. This perpetuates negative thoughts and emotions with an intense emphasis that forces one to assimilate, assess, and examine ourselves (and also others). That's one of the reasons why it is so important to learn how to deal with envy.

Talking will make our envy even worse by flooding our ears with allegations and antagonistic remarks. It is, in fact, ever easier to live with what our basic internal voice informs us about our condition than the actual circumstance. The rejection or double-crossing of our mate is disruptive. Yet, all the horrible muses that our basic internal voice informs us about after the mishap are what regularly disturbs us much more. "You're such an insane person. Have you at any point contemplated why you should be playful? You're going to end up there. You're never going to trust any person." To explain how this inner adversary drives our negative thoughts toward envy, we're going to make a jackass of two kinds of jealousy: casual jealousy and severe jealousy. Even though these two kinds of jealousy meet regularly, their unique investigation will help us see how jealousy affects different parts of our lives and how we are all the more likely to adapt to jealousy.

Romantic Jealousy

It is a straightforward truth that as a relationship is getting more grounded, partners aren't, in effect, excessively jealous. On the contrary, the happier we should be, the more we cling to and recognize our envy's feelings, apart from our mate. Our jealousy likewise originates from our dread of being deluded, harmed, or terminated. In any relationship, regardless of the conditions, except if we manage this inclination inside ourselves, we will probably succumb to sentiments of jealousy, doubt, or weakness.

Such critical contemplation about ourselves results from encounters of early life. We also convey feelings about ourselves that our folks or essential family members have towards themselves or us. Furthermore, unknowingly, we replay, reproduce, or respond to old, normal examples in our present relationships. For example, if we feel set as children, we would effortlessly see our partners reject us. Instead, we may pick a progressively troublesome partner or even hold fast to activities that drive our partner away.

How much we, as kids, received self-basic mentalities likewise influences how much our delicate internal voice, especially in our relationships, will impact our grown-up lives. Also, regardless of our particular perspectives, we as a whole hold the internal evaluation somewhat. Any of us will identify with deduction. We will not be chosen. The level to which we expect this powerlessness is affecting how we feel awkward in a relationship.

At the point when our most noticeably terrible considerations work out as expected when we find out about a companion's cheating, we, despite everything, react by changing annoyance to ourselves as "stupid, unlovable, demolished, or rejected." Like a cruel guide, our basic internal voice cautions us not to trust or feel excessively powerless. This gives us the feeling we are unlovable and not prepared for marriage. It is the delicate murmur that spreads suspicion, disarray, and doubt. "For what reason accomplishes she work late?" "For what reason does his better half pick him over me?" "What will she do when I'm away?" "For what reason does she give an excessive amount of consideration to what she's expressing?" We know how jealousy functions comprehend that these feelings will gradually start to grow and bloom into a lot greater, progressively imbued attacks on ourselves and our companion. "She will not hang with you. There must be anybody better." "He's lost intrigue. He needs to flee from you." "Who'd tune in? You're so exhausting."

How to Deal with Jealousy

Acknowledge It

It is natural to feel ashamed about being jealous, but do not deny or ignore it. Indeed, you can't neglect a wound and expect it to heal; you'll have to get immediate medical attention. Likewise, you need to be honest about your feelings and acknowledge your jealousy before you can heal. Begin with acknowledging how your insecurities make you feel and how they are damaging your relationship. It is often easier said than act upon, but it is the first step in the right direction.

Consider What's Going on

Daniel Siegel uses the word "sift" to explain how we can "sift" through the emotions, images, feelings, and thoughts that come up when we focus on certain things in our lives. When we feel angry, that's what we should want to do. We're trying to discover what jealousy is pulling from observations, images, feelings, and ideas. Is the present condition within the household, which creates the old complicated or long-lived, deteriorating selfperception? The more we can connect those emotions or overreactions to earlier events that first created them, the happier we will be with our present situation.

Discover Your Insecurities

If you've noticed that you are overly jealous, you need to discover the cause and deal with it. How do you do this? Ninety percent of the time, jealousy springs from insecurities, so make a list of your insecurities. For example, do you look down on yourself? Do you wonder why your partner is still with you? Do you continuously feel other people are better than you? When you do this, you'll gain control over how you respond to these weaknesses and start working on them.

Calm Down

We'll find opportunities to re-emerge and unwind, no matter how confused we might be. Most notably, we're going to do so by capturing our emotions of sympathy. No matter how amazing we feel, keep in mind our feelings prop up through waves, first developing and then dying. We will be mindful of our jealousy and accept it without any follow-up. First of all, we can learn methodologies to calm down before we react by going for a walk or a succession of breaths. It is much easier to calm down along these lines because we should not welcome or participate in the angry expressions of our inward adversaries because it is essential to find a way to demoralize them. When we do so, we're going to stand up for ourselves and other people we care for and be honest and transparent about how we react.

Use Your Jealousy as an Opportunity

Besides being the giant green monster that destroys love, jealousy can be a means for clarity. You see, feelings of jealousy are stirred up because of a relationship problem, either from you or your partner. So, you need to closely look at the jealous behavior you're portraying and ask what that jealousy is attempting to solve.

For instance, if jealousy springs up because your partner broke your trust in the past and created an opportunity for doubt to creep in, your jealousy is not the problem. Instead, your partner's breach of trust is the real problem. Moreover, if you're taking out your insecurity on your partner, then insecurity is the problem.

You need to look at your jealousy as an opportunity to solve a problem.

Focus on making sure you and your partner have no reason to be jealous.

Work on Your Self-Esteem

After discovering your insecurities and making a list of the feelings that fuel your jealousy, prescribe a solution for each of them. You might discover that you've been comparing yourself to your partner's ex and have been feeling inadequate. To remedy this, write down all your good qualities and everything your partner loves about you. Do the same for every insecurity; afterward, isolate yourself from anything that makes you feel inferior. If you're following celebrities whose achievements intimidate you, unfollow them until you get your confidence back.

Find the Cause of the Problem

Is your insecurity or jealousy caused by unhealed wounds from your past? Some people struggle with jealousy because of the traumatic childhood experience they had. Others might be insecure because of a defect or an addiction. No matter what it is, get to the root of that feeling of jealousy, and get professional help to enable you to deal with the toxic feelings for good.

Well, since the beginning of time, jealousy is an emotion as prevalent as love. Whether it's intentional or not, it stays in our relationships with the people we love. But only if we were fully aware of what is being kept at stake that we would make the best of efforts to shy away from that poisonous feeling. This inevitable feeling finds its habitat in all of us; however, it's because most of us stay silent about it that it stays within its boundaries. It's only when you start acting upon your feelings and thoughts that you start digging the grave of your own relationship. So, while it is an established fact that jealousy sustains in every relationship, a question that emerges is, where does it come from?

When it comes to understanding the triggers, it's vital to perceive that jealousy is more associated with your vulnerabilities than your partner's actions. If you encounter thoughts such as "He was extra friendly with his assistant. He's probably having an affair with her." Or "She met her ex today; she is obviously attached to him till now." Well, you can create all the movies in your head and stretch them to whatever limits you like; however, you need to keep in mind that these are still movies and probably have no connection to the non-fictional world that we call reality. These feelings might have strong relevance to your past. An incident that embedded insecurities deep in you is hard to let go of and move on. If you've been abandoned or betrayed before, you're left with a deep scar that gets alive every time you feel something similar happening. You might find love again in your life, but this enrooted feeling of fear and insecurity lingers on with you in the form of jealousy. Now, as this can be just as disastrous for your partner as for you, it's better to talk to them about your past, rant it all out, and move on from it. It's only when you're able to detach yourself from the trauma that you stop carrying the baggage with you everywhere. And the sooner you let it off your chest, the lighter you will feel and the prosperous it would be for your relationship. More than anything, it would allow your partner to understand the reason behind your behavior, be mindful of the triggers and respect them.

Another factor that gives birth to jealousy within your relationship is low self-esteem. The feeling that you're not worthy of being loved, why would anyone love someone like you or thinking that no one values you. It's hard for you to believe your partner's feelings towards you. All it does is make you question their expression of love. You would keep infusing yourself with the dubious thoughts that your partner is lying or keeping your heart. This might rev up from the loop of self-criticism that believes that you're not goodlooking enough, and so no guy can ever fall for you. Thinking of that would always keep you complex and insecure whenever a good-looking person surrounds your partner. Again, it hoists the unhealthy facet of distrustfulness that never drives its way towards success.

Another thing that you must always bear in mind is that no one has a "movie love"; there is nothing like that. Whatever you've grown up watching on TV, the romance and love-at-first-sight, the cuteness is all limited to the screen that fills the colors. Everything outside that screen is a completely different story that has nothing to do with the fairytale you just watched and admired. There is no knight in real life, there is no white horse, and you're definitely not a princess to be rescued; therefore, keep your eye on the very fine line that distinguishes between fiction and reality. This is actually one of the most significant root causes of jealousy. People watch romantic movies and begin building castles in the air about them meeting a guy just like the protagonist in the movie that would treat them like a queen. Well, if there's one out there who can treat you like a queen, then that's you, so do that for yourself. This in no way means real love doesn't exist; it for sure does. It is just nothing like the film that kept your jaw dropped open and your eyes filled with awe. These unrealistic scenes make people set hallmarks of expectations that a real-world hero can't meet, and once that happens, you start overthinking and feeling insecure, which leads to problems. Real love is practical; it requires understanding and compromise. Your partner can't stay with you a hundred percent of the time, nor can they talk to you at all hours. And more so, it isn't even healthy for two people to spend the entire time together. At the same time, people also expect their partner to give away the life they had before them and merge their existence into theirs. Expecting them to do that is close to impossible. And even if you compel them into doing so, you'll just be suffocating them into a box that doesn't feel like home at all. They'd be forced to live there and pretend to be a person that they are not. A person that you can't be themselves marks a life of pretense, which is terrible beyond expression. There must always be a healthy amount of space between you two to help your bond sustain. Once you're clear of what to expect, you are no longer face to face with disappointments, which eradicates jealousy and keeps your bond fortified.

Do you qualify yourself as competitive? Are you constantly putting yourself in fierce competition with your friends and partner? This trait of yours can be a significant cause of jealousy in your relationships. Having a competitive spirit is good, but letting it interfere with your interpersonal emotions can be hurtful. This is because you find yourself incapable of being happy with the other person's achievements or accomplishments. The angle of your perception sees them getting ahead of you while you were the slow one, enraging jealousy inside you. This gives your self-esteem a beating, leads towards self-scrutiny, and results in excessive overthinking. Remember, love means to be happy in the other person's success, see it as your own, and celebrate it with the utmost optimism. However, a competitor finds it challenging to inculcate those feelings in them, thus ruining the vibe. To make it worse, your feelings are very much judgeable by the other person, making them uncomfortable for sharing their success stories with you. Hence, another barrier that keeps your partner at an arm's distance. All of this together can be highly problematic for both of you. Whether it's a friend, a sibling, or a spouse, an unproductive competitive spirit can tend to create issues beyond your comprehension.

This is also subtly interrelated to perfectionism. A person with perfectionist qualities keeps comparing themselves to other people, finding the qualities that they don't possess. This hoists jealousy as you fear them being better than you in certain aspects and being preferred over you. No matter who the person you're comparing yourself to is, it's unhealthy for your cognition as well as your partner's. Mainly because this entire story of them wanting to choose the other person over you is all knitted in your head and has absolutely nothing to do with your thoughts. Having a baseless argument over this can be exhausting and agitating, burning the fire of resentment in between you two and pulling you apart. If you've often witnessed yourself looking at other people during a party and observed women who're more gorgeous than you, smarter than you, or funnier than you and thought that your partner would consider their personality over yours, that's an unhealthy indication towards the spiking up of jealousy. A simple fact that can make your life a hundred times easier is accepting the fact that there's always going to be that one person who's better than you. But that isn't what matters; what matters is if your partner would actually leave and choose them. Ask yourself that question and demand an honest answer; if your inner self replies with a "No," then you've got nothing to worry about; if the answer is affirmative, then you should be wise enough to choose what's best in your interests.

Another aspect that brings jealousy to the surface is the dynamics of your relationship. Every relationship has a unique quality that sets the tone of your behavior. Some people are more prone to jealousy than others. And naturally, one is more likely to feel jealous in an unstable relationship. If you're involved in a romantic relationship where you deal with frequent breakups or recurring fights, then you'd find yourself trapped in a bubble of doubts and perplexities of whether they have authentic feelings for you or not. You'd be way more scared of losing the other person, which boosts jealousy and makes it more explosive. Many relationships that are already had enough and are on the last drops of oxygen might find jealousy as the last nail. If you're someone who has a mismatched attachment style with your partner, then your relationship would fall victim to jealousy way more quickly. For example, if your spouse likes to have their own personal space while you require constant attention and reassurance, then you're very much likely to feel jealous. For example, an overly outgoing husband might make his introverted wife jealous of his meets and greets. Having a totally different nature causes clashes in the way you deal with your partner and can ignite bitterness, which harms the overall impression of your bond.

Projection is a considerable cause of jealousy. Things that happen to us in our lives prompt the thought that they might be going on with our partners as well, which leads to keeping tabs and asking their whereabouts every now and then. You might have been scared of your partner being attracted to a coworker, but have you ever thought about where the perception came from? Was it because you feel attracted to one of your colleagues as well? This is a known fact that most of our fears about other people come from the actions that we ourselves are guilty about. Things that we know we shouldn't have done instill the fears of being done to us. Cheating doesn't hurt as much as being cheated on does, and that implies every wrongdoing that we do, whether intentional or unintentional. You get scared of being hurt, heartbroken, or left, and so you take all the precautionary measures to protect yourself and prevent that from happening. You question every encounter they had with the opposite sex, check their emails, eavesdrop on their calls, reassure their feelings, observe their ignorance, and jump to the conclusion within an instant. In this case, the elevation of jealousy has no connection to your partner's doings but your own.

Watching your partner struggle with anxiety can be very difficult. But if you don't know how to help them, you will feel helpless, too. If you don't really understand what your partner is going through and you only
see them struggling, you might do things that can make the situation worse. Over time, your relationship will start deteriorating until you are left with a broken bond and a person whom you don't know anymore.

Not knowing how to help your partner can leave you feeling sad, frustrated, or even angry. Meanwhile, when your partner doesn't see any effort from you, they may feel isolated, lonely, and have other negative feelings that can worsen their condition. You obviously want to learn how to help your partner and save your relationship.

To have the capacity to help your partner deal with their condition, you must first educate yourself. This is what you are doing now. You have already learned what anxiety is, the common signs that may indicate that your partner is struggling with it, and how you can communicate more effectively with them. But we aren't done yet! There's still a lot to identify before you can apply your knowledge to your real-life situations. Finding out everything you can about anxiety will help you learn more about the condition. This, in turn, allows you to understand your partner better as they face their anxiety. When your partner sees that you want to help them, this can make them feel inspired to help themselves. Then this will awaken your desire to work together as you share the common goal of learning how to manage your partner's anxiety effectively.

Recognizing Panic Attacks and Other Irrational Behaviors
These days, it seems like anxiety disorders have become very common. Among the different stages of anxiety, a lot of people seem to reach paniclevel anxiety, and when this happens, they experience an anxiety attack. An anxiety attack happens when a person gets an overwhelming feeling of fear, distress, apprehension, or worry and they don't know how to overcome it. For some people, this attack comes gradually, but for others, it comes on suddenly and with incredible intensity. While the symptoms of this attack may vary, the most common ones are:

- Feeling dizzy, worried, restless, apprehensive, or fearful.
- Dry mouth.
- Shortness of breath.
- Excessive sweating.
- Hot flashes or cold chills.
- Tingling or numbness.

Another kind of "attack" that someone with anxiety may experience is a panic attack. A panic attack is similar to an anxiety attack, but it has different causes, including stress, chemical imbalances, using drugs or caffeine, and even heredity. Panic attacks also occur when someone has a mental disorder such as anxiety. If this is something that occurs to your partner, you must learn how to help them get through the attack. Here are some tips:

- Help your partner realize that the symptoms they feel aren't harmful or dangerous. To your partner, these symptoms are exaggerated, which makes them feel frightened. Therefore, you should try to explain things to them in the gentlest and calmest way possible.

- Help your partner identify their feelings. This lessens the intensity of those feelings.

- Try not to add to the panic your partner feels by asking them questions like, "What are you so worried about?"

- Help your partner focus on the present. Talk your partner through the current situation so they don't worry about what might happen in the future.

- Distract your partner with a simple activity, like asking them to count backward, clap your hands with a specific rhythm and ask them to follow it, and other things that can help take their mind off their anxious thoughts.

Some of these strategies may work well for your partner, while others won't. Try out different techniques until you find those that are most effective. Some of these may even work to help your partner deal with anxiety attacks, too. The key here is to help your partner overcome the attack without succumbing to it.

Generally, feelings of anxiety can emerge when something triggers them. There are so many possible triggers, and these triggers may vary from one person to another. Some people may have a single trigger, while others have several. Also, some people may react severely to certain triggers while others need a higher level of exposure before, they are affected. Either way, some of the most common triggers of people who suffer from anxiety disorders are the following:

- Caffeine.

- Conflict.

- Financial problems.

- Health problems.

- Medications or drugs.

- Negative thoughts.

- Public performances or events.

- Personal triggers.

- Skipping meals.

- Social events or parties.

- Stress.

Also, in some cases, you might be your partner's trigger. If this is the case, aim not to take it personally. Continue being supportive and loving, even if you find out that your partner's anxiety gets triggered when you're around. In such a case, though, try to find out why you have become your partner's trigger. Communicate with your partner and ask them questions to get to the bottom of things. After all, you can't help your partner if your mere presence sets off their anxiety.

Then, there are nervous breakdowns. People with anxiety are more susceptible to having them, but the good news is, you can help prevent this from happening if you can catch it early. As you observe your partner for anxiety attacks, panic attacks, and general anxious feelings, try to recognize the signs of an impending nervous breakdown, too. Here are the most common signs:

- Unexplained changes in their appetite.
- Changes in their grooming and sleeping habits.
- Changes in their mood or energy levels.
- Frequently feeling weak or fatigued.
- Frequent muscle aches and headaches.
- Breathing difficulties.
- Having inappropriate reactions to interactions and events.
- Not wanting to socialize with other people.
- Issues with their memory, organization, and attention.
- Gastrointestinal and sexual function problems.

- Substance or drug use.
- Sudden weight loss or weight gain.

If you realize more than one of these signs in a partner who suffers from anxiety, then a nervous breakdown might not be far behind. When this happens, your partner will lose their ability to function altogether. Therefore, you must take the necessary steps to snap your partner out of it. Do this by helping them deal with their problems or lightening their load.

What Can You Do About It?

Whether it's dealing with panic attacks or the anxiety disorder itself, there are several things you can do to help your partner out. After learning about their condition and knowing how to identify the "danger signs," the next thing to do is to learn to help them deal with it. Here are some ways you can do to make things easier for your partner and yourself:

Learn to Accept Your Partner's Condition

Acceptance is key when you find out that your partner has a mental condition such as an anxiety disorder. If you cannot accept this, you won't be willing to help them out. Whether your partner told you about their condition or you found out yourself (and your partner confirmed it), learn how to accept this diagnosis. It may be difficult, especially if your partner developed the condition recently, but acceptance must come to you. Once you can accept that your partner is suffering from an anxiety disorder, then you can take the next steps.

Set Boundaries in Your Relationship

Since your goal is to empower your partner, it's important to set clear boundaries. Before doing this, take some time to learn more about your partner's condition and how they are coping with it. For instance, if you see that your partner is trying hard to manage their condition, then you won't have to set boundaries that are particularly strict. However, if your partner is becoming too dependent on you, this is when setting boundaries becomes essential. Just make sure to communicate these boundaries in the gentlest, most positive way so your partner won't take things the wrong way.

Focus on Your Own Self-Care

Helping your partner is a noble thing, but in the process, you shouldn't forget to care for yourself, too. Don't offer so much of yourself that you have nothing left. Remember, if you end up developing anxiety because you have invested so much in helping your partner, you might be the one who gets a nervous breakdown. Practice physical, emotional, and mental self-care so you can remain strong enough to support your partner through their difficult times.

Take Time to Relax Together

As you are dealing with an issue or a challenge in your relationship, try to find enjoyable things to do, too. Take the time to relax together as you did before this condition came into your relationship and made it more complicated. Try taking a spa day together, practice couples' meditation, or just take turns massaging each other. Doing relaxing things together makes your bond stronger and it can help alleviate your partner's anxiety.

Come Up With a Backup Plan for Dealing with Situations

Helping your partner deal with anxiety involves coming up with a plan that includes effective strategies to get through difficult situations. However, even if you plan everything well, unexpected things might still happen. For instance, when you attend a party with your partner, you can prepare for it by doing a relaxing activity first. But once you get there, your partner's anxiety might kick in which, in turn, might lead to an anxiety or panic attack. In such cases, you should always have a backup plan. You can either involve your partner in creating these backup plans or establish them yourself. As long as you have an alternative solution to dealing with difficult situations, you can help your partner get through the most unexpected events.

Mindful Practices

To quote Jon Kabat-Zinn, "Mindfulness means paying attention in a particular way: on purpose, in the present moment, and non-judgmentally."

Another definition comes from Scott Bishop, who is a psychologist. He describes being mindful as a present-centered, nonjudgmental, elaborate awareness where every sensation, feeling, and thought that comes up is acknowledged and accepted for what it is.

This might sound simple, but mindfulness can change the way we relate to experiences and events. It can create a better way of living in the world that will make us happier and less reactive.

Why Should You Practice Mindfulness?

For many people practicing mindfulness is an excellent way to enhance their performance or health. Other people use it to explore themselves. And still, others use it as a part of their spirituality to bring them closer to their "divine truth."

It doesn't matter what a person's motivation is; research has shown that practicing mindfulness can change the brain's functions and structure and change how we respond to stress. This suggests that mindfulness can greatly impact our emotional and physical health that would be worth looking at.

CBT and Mindfulness

CBT commonly uses mindfulness. This is known as mindfulness-based cognitive therapy or MBCT. It is a type of psychotherapy that combines meditation, cognitive therapy, and the cultivation of a present-oriented attitude known as mindfulness.

Cognitive therapy's main assumption is that thoughts come before moods and that having false self-beliefs will create negative emotions. Cognitive therapy's main goal is to help you reassess and recognize your negative thought patterns and replace them that are more positive and closer to reality.

Mindfulness-based cognitive therapy will build upon these basic principles by using mindfulness meditation to help people pay more attention to their feelings and thoughts without judging them.

For example, a person who has chronic depression can use mindfulness to avoid relapses by learning how to not engage with their automatic thought patterns that cause their depression to become worse. It has been proven that mindfulness can, on average, reduce the risk of a depression relapse by 50%, no matter the person's education, age, sex, or relationship status.

Mindfulness and Stress

Mindfulness is also a powerful tool for reducing stress, which we've already discussed everybody has. There is growing evidence from numerous studies done by hundreds of universities that show mindfulness helps to gently build inner strength so that future stressors don't have a strong impact on our physical and mental wellbeing.

Why is mindfulness so great for stress? Here are nine reasons why.

1.   You notice your thoughts – You will learn how to take a step back from your thoughts and not take them literally. This will prevent your stress response from being initiated.

2.   You won't immediately react to a situation – Instead, you will find you have a moment to stop and think and reach a healthy solution.

3.   Mindfulness will switch on your "being" mode – This mode is closely connected with relaxation. The opposite of this is your "doing" mode and is connected with your stress response.

4.   You become more aware of your needs – You might notice a pain quicker and take the correct course of action.

5.   You notice others' emotions – As you increase your emotional intelligence, you are less likely to face conflicts.

6.   Your level of compassion and care for yourself and others grow – A compassionate mind helps to inhibit and soothe the stress response.

7.   Mindfulness reduces brain activity in the amygdale – The amygdale is a big player in your stress response, so your stress will be reduced.

8. You can focus better – This will help you do your work more efficiently, and it will improve your sense of well-being and lowers your stress response.

9. You can change your attitude to stress – Instead of only seeing the negative consequences of feeling stressed, mindfulness will provide you an area of space to think differently about stress.

Mindfulness Can Be Developed in Various Ways

If mindfulness is so helpful, how can people learn to develop this skill? Various practices help support developing mindfulness, including being in nature, movement, and meditation. This chapter describes some of these meditation techniques, but generally, they try to develop the three main characteristics of mindfulness:

• An attitude that is kind, curious, and doesn't judge

• Attention to the things that are happening around you

• Intention to create awareness

To help you cultivate a mindfulness practice, the following are some various ways to help cultivate mindfulness. It is helpful to use mindfulness along with the other techniques that are discussed in this book. It all works together to help improve your mental wellbeing.

Mindful Breathing to Begin Your Day

Set your alarm clock for either five or ten minutes earlier than when you typically get up. Once the alarm goes off, sit up and get comfortable. You are going to use this time to enjoy some centering breathing. This is one of the best ways to start your day. You will be getting up at the right time, and you aren't sacrificing any time from your normal routine. When you practice mindfulness during morning hours, you are starting your day feeling clearheaded, refreshed, and calm. It allows you to wake up instead of jumping right out of bed and having to rush around right from the start gently.

You can close your eyes if you would like. When I keep my eyes open, I find that I need to take care of that just defeats the whole purpose of this exercise. Breathe in deeply and notice the sensation of your breath filling your lungs. Breathe out, and breathe in again. You might realize your mind wanders off here and there, but that is okay. Just gently bring it back to your breath.

With some time and practice, this will get easier. You can set a timer for five or ten minutes. You don't need to do this longer than that.

Pick A Task To Mindfully Do

You probably have a page full of things you would like to get done. Those tasks give you the best chance to bring more mindfulness into your life.

Look at these ideas:

- Take a walk while mindfully noticing all of the sounds that are happening around you. Notice how the ground feels as you are walking,or look for things that you may have never seen before.

- Take a mindful shower by observing the sensations of the water running down your body.

- Drink your morning coffee or tea mindfully. This means that you will need to put your phone away and then notice its tastes, temperature, flavor, and aroma.

The idea of doing this activity is to start creating a habit of doing something that is simple, that you would already be doing every day, but in a new, mindful way. Release all of the distractions as your work to focus on the present moment.

Allow Yourself To Feel Your Emotions Without Judging Them

This is a great activity to take part in at the end of the day and check in on your needs. You can do this simply by asking yourself, "How am I feeling right now?" If you can, try to give yourself a couple of minutes each day to observe your emotions while creating a space where you can experience them.

You could find a quiet place and focus all of your attention inside of you.

Take a moment to notice how you physically feel.

Think about the events that happened to you that day.

Notice any emotions you might have and why they are there.

Now, release those reasons and focus solely on the emotion. You might encounter something like: "I feel irritated because the house is a mess and my boss expects too much out of me." You can break this down into: "I feel irritated."

Notice how it feels to be irritated without judging yourself for that feeling.

Let yourself really feel that emotion, and it might be fading away.

Have a Mindful Conversation With Someone You Love

Connecting with others is key to feeling heard, supported, and loved. Why not make a point of adding some mindfulness into your relationship to bring the two of you closer? Here is how you can do this:

- Ask someone you love if they have time to talk. Tell them that you would really like to hear how their week was and let them know that you want to have a conversation with them without distractions like phones or television.

- You can also decide to go out to someplace nice like a restaurant where you can have something to eat and talk about, or you could just for a walk.

- You intend to give your attention and time to your loved ones while being open-minded while they are talking.

- When you have finished talking, compliment the person. Tell them that you appreciate their openness, honesty, and time.

Do Something Creative

Coloring, play an instrument, plan a trip, build things, sew, cook, write, garden, or paint… there are so many ways you can express your creativity.

Anytime you can immerse yourself into a creative activity, you are experiencing mindfulness. You don't think about anything but what you are doing at that moment because you are too focused on taking part in the activity.

The other week I decided to plant some new tulip bulbs. I headed out to the garden and placed the bulbs on top of the ground to see if I liked where they were placed. It took me a couple of times to get them exactly how I wanted them. I wasn't thinking about my unread emails, what I would cook for dinner, or thinking about that to-do list hanging on the fridge. I was only paying attention to my flowers I would enjoy in the spring. I was completely immersed in gardening. While we are on the subject of nature:

Spend Some Time In Nature

When you are out in nature, it isn't just a great way to add some mindfulness into your world, but you get to experience numerous other benefits, too.

One study done in 2019 discovered that spending only two hours outside every week could help with a person's wellbeing and health. This study involved more than 20,000 participants, and those who spent two hours in nature didn't experience mental health disorders or poor health such as cardiovascular disease and obesity. The time that they spent in nature didn't even have to be physical. It could be as simple as sitting on a park bench and just enjoying the view.

Another study showed that spending 20 minutes in nature could lower a person's stress hormone levels. Making a point to spend some time in nature will help your physical and mental health. The following are some great ways to get out in nature:

- Horseback riding
- Go paddle-boarding
- Go to a farm and pick berries
- Walk around a botanical garden
- Sit under a tree
- Hike to a waterfall
- Walk around a lake

There are numerous things that you can do in nature. Basically, you just need to get out and enjoy it.

Every day when we get up it is very important to "program" body and mind face the challenge of a new day and the opportunity we have to feel good and live happily.

Our mind has awesome power and can perform all those tasks we indicate with great confidence. It is important to infuse us with high doses of positivism and try to see the positive aspect of things. Even if it seems a difficult experience to overcome, getting used to this habit will benefit us.

When sad emotions and thoughts try to take control of our life and health, we need to take a few minutes to reflect and ponder whether it is worth wasting our energy on such thoughts.

The most likely outcome of this exercise is that, instead of complaining and allowing ourselves to be dominated by these emotions, we want and try to change our lives, to seek solutions, so that this negativity does not degrade their quality.

It is scientifically proven that positivism and emotions such as cheerfulness, happiness, and a smile release hormones responsible for strengthening our immune system.

Likewise, it has been verified that negative emotions can act in the opposite way, causing a weakening of our body's defenses and making our body more prone to contract various diseases.

It is important to try not to demonize negativity—it is about processing and dealing with it. There are some obvious solutions, such as eliminating toxic people from our lives and focusing on activities that make us feel good. Let's see together some useful and effective steps to manage our negative thoughts better:

- Let's observe our body language. Are we hunched over, bent over, or with closed shoulders? Do we tend to close our bodies? Improper body language can lower self-esteem and lead to a lack of confidence. In this emotional state, it is natural to start having negative thoughts. Let's open the posture and learn to smile more. Experts have confirmed that by correcting body language the mind adapts accordingly. So, let's try to correct the posture, open the shoulders and smile more often. It may be just what we need to start clearing negative thoughts.

- Sometimes a negative thought occurs because there are problems or emotions that we need to communicate and need to be expressed. It is never good to keep everything inside because we risk accumulating negativity and discontent, up to burst in the worst possible ways. Let's talk about our negative thoughts! Turning thoughts into words shapes them and makes them visible, helping us put problems into perspective and deal with them more effectively. It also often helps us to realize how much we magnify the problems in our heads.

- When the mind gets out of control, it may be difficult to stay calm. In this whirlwind of emotions, it is much more difficult to keep the flow of thoughts under control, especially the negative ones. Five minutes of awareness and concentration every day are often enough to begin identifying thoughts, cataloging them, and, if necessary, moving them away to enjoy a few moments of total peace of mind. Meditation can help this situation. Just five minutes a day can be extremely useful to free our minds.

- Negative thinking is sometimes the result of a distorted perspective or prejudices that we have carried with us for years. Let's change the focus of our thoughts! For example, instead of thinking "I'm having a hard time and I have problems," we might think "I'm facing some challenges, but I'm working to find solutions." Basically, we are saying the same thing, but in the second statement, the meaning is positive.

- When negative thoughts come, finding a creative outlet to get them out of our heads is very useful. Let's try to write, draw or color, or find a manual hobby.

- Sometimes our thoughts are a product of our environment. For example, if negative people surround us, we are likely to start thinking negatively too. Getting away from this environment can be of great help and will prove to be extremely therapeutic.

- Sometimes, in the daily routine, we lose sight of the beautiful things present in our lives. Let's train our minds to return to focus on all the good that happens around us by exercising gratitude. Let's make a list of all the beautiful things that are part of our life, even the smallest ones, without taking anything for granted. The wonderful things in life are often right in front of our eyes, and we just can't see them.

- It's easy to fall into the trap of negative thoughts when focusing on what people might say or think about us and what we do. In this way, we nullify our personal power by putting it in others' hands. It is curious, but true, that almost everyone does not have much time, attention, or energy to think or talk about what we do. This awareness can help us remove harmful patterns, allowing us to take small steps towards what is truly important to us.

- Let's question the negative thoughts that creep into our minds! It can be simply an episode of fatigue, or we are overworked, and here comes the negativity to cloud our minds. Let's not focus on a small mistake or on a bad day—let's instead focus on the other 95% of our life that tends to be positive.

- As we have already said, the environment in which we live greatly influences our thoughts. What are the three main sources of negativity in our life? It could be people, websites, television, magazines, social networks, and so on. Let's ask ourselves what we can do to limit the time we expose ourselves to these sources; let's take small steps and focus on just one of these sources and dedicate the time we have to more positive people or activities.

Negative thoughts represent something that each of us has to fight against, but instead of getting angry, let's accept these feelings and try to overcome them.

Let's find peace of mind, take back our personal power and take advantage of all the benefits that optimism and positive thinking can bring to our life.

Health

Attaining bodily health is generally connected with keeping a healthful lifestyle; ingesting healthful meals, exercising often, in addition to taking good and enough rest, all of those and more do contribute to sound health. However, health does not only mean a person's physical health but additionally his/her mental, social and emotional health. It is stated to be approximately the whole wellness of a human being.

Healthy Lifestyle

A wholesome and healthy lifestyle is our routine and the way we live our lives; Do we worry about sports or eat food or materials that might be dangerous for us? If yes, then we're a long way from residing a wholesome lifestyle. This is what ensures a blooming frame system, it normally improves the fitness and wellness of an individual.

A healthful lifestyle is a manner of dwelling that lowers the threat of being severely unwell or demise early. Not all sicknesses are preventable, however, a big percentage of deaths, mainly the ones from coronary heart sickness and lung cancer, can be avoided. Scientific research has recognized positive sorts of behavior that contribute to the improvement of non-communicable sicknesses and early death. Health isn't pretty much fending off sickness. It is likewise approximately physical, intellectual, and social well-being. When a healthful lifestyle is adopted, a more positive version is supplied for different humans within the family, mainly children as role models and mentors. Healthy living aims to assist people in changing their mentality and their behavior, as well as enhance their fitness to stay healthier, longer lives.

Mental and physical fitness are possibly the 2 maximums regularly mentioned varieties of fitness.

Spiritual, emotional, and financial health additionally make contributions to overall well-being. Medical specialists have related those to decreased stress levels and progressed mental and physical well-being.

People with good financial health, for example, may also have little worries about their income and have the means to shop for clean and healthier meals regularly. Those with suitable spiritual health may also sense an experience of calm and reason that fuels their spiritual and mental health. Therefore, the overall state of mind contributes largely to how healthy a person can be. However, if you want to leave a healthy lifestyle, you have to work on your mindset, as it is a very powerful tool in improving your well-being.

The Mind

The mind, they say, is a very powerful place. It's where we process our thoughts before starting with action.

Our thoughts shape and affect how we perceive things and what we want. When we reason properly, we're stimulated to do things that are sensible and encouraged to behave in methods that assist as opposed to damage ourselves and others.

At the same time, strong feelings or emotions impact our thoughts and assist or avoid how properly we reason in a situation. At any given moment, our minds (the complex of internal thoughts, emotions, and goals) can be swayed by our ability to reason and process information.

Healthy living starts with the mind. Without a clear mindset, it will be difficult for one to start living healthy, or even if we start, it will be difficult to maintain in the long run. We have to be positive, examine, and tell ourselves we can do it. If you believe you can succeed, then go for it, you're halfway through your journey of a healthy life.

Mastering Your Mind

Mastering the mind may be one of the most complex but most worthwhile equipment to achieve a fulfilling life. It is viable to be the master of your mind, however, how regularly do you put into effect your extraordinary strength to do so?

The standard of our mind plays an important role in determining the standard of our lives. That's how critical it is to inspire a disciplined mindset towards tracking our mind and ensuring we fill ourselves with positivity instead of negative and toxic thoughts.

Positive and Negative Mindset

People with positive thoughts are typically empowered to reap their goals. On the contrary, negative thoughts can weigh us down, bringing fears and doubts to stop us from making the changes that could move us towards our goals.

It is essential to understand our negative thoughts and not to bury them as they may have a subconscious effect on our actions. It should be understood that these thoughts are proscribing or removing the opportunities one could have.

Positive thinking does not indicate putting up a strong face and ignoring life's unpleasant circumstances. Positive thinking simply means approaching stressful situations more positively and prolifically. You are optimistic the best, not the worst, to happen.

Self-thoughts are a common starting point for positive thinking. The infinite stream of unspoken words that run through your mind is known as selfthought. These automated thoughts may be positive or negative. Any way of thinking about yourself comes from common sense and reason. Other selfthought might also additionally stand up from misconceptions that you create due to the inadequate amount of information.

If the mind that runs thru your head is typically negative, your outlook on lifestyles is much more likely pessimistic. If your thoughts are typically affirmative, you're probably an optimist — a person who practices positive thinking.

Effects of Positive Thoughts on Our Health
Researchers keep discovering the outcomes of positivity and optimism on health. **Health advantages that positive thinking may also offer include:**

- Lower case of depression.

- Better coping abilities during the duration of hardships and stress instances.

- Lower distress degrees and depression.

- Greater resistance to cold.

- Better cardiovascular fitness and decreased chance of death from cardiovascular disease.

- Better mental and bodily well-being Increase in lifespan.

It is uncertain why individuals who engage in positive thoughts have these fitness benefits. One concept is that having an advantageous outlook allows you to manage higher with stressful situations, which reduces the dangerous outcomes of pressure on your body and health.

Additionally, it gives the idea that advantageous and optimistic humans beings generally tend to have healthier lifestyles — they engage in more extra bodily activity, observe a better diet, and don't smoke or drink alcohol excessively.

Identifying Bad Thinking

If you are not sure if your self-thought is advantageous or bad? Some not frequent types of negative thinkings include:

Catastrophizing

You usually expect the worst. For instance, you probably are in a hurry to meet a deadline and you accidentally hit an animal and, so you routinely assume that the rest of your day could be a disaster.

Filtering

You enlarge the bad instances of a situation and filter all the advantageous or good ones. For example, you had a fantastic day at work. You finished your obligations in advance of time and have been complimented for doing a rapid and thorough job. That night, your cognizance is best in your plan to do even greater obligations and overlook approximately the compliments you received. You feel you need to do more or prove a point. You feel you're not still good enough and only see your mistakes and not your strengths.

Personalizing

When something awful occurs, you usually blame yourself. For example, you meet a group of friends to discuss some ideas and yours doesn't get picked, and also you just conclude that the reason for your idea not being picked is due to the fact nobody sees you as smart enough.

You only see things in 2 ways: nice or terrible. There is no such thing as a middle ground. You think you must be flawless or you will be a complete failure. An example is a student that gets the second position but gets upset because he/she feels being second best is not good enough and he/she has to be the best at all times.

Focus On Positive Thoughts

Focus on positive thinking. You can learn to turn negative thinking into positive thinking. The process is simple, but it takes time and practice. Finally, you have to develop new habits. These are some ways to think and act more positively, as well as optimistically.

Method

Entering into an afternoon with something nice is crucial. Start your day with expressions of gratitude. Begin your days with a way of being grateful for something you already have. It will be as easy as waking up and creating a conscious announcement which you are thankful to be awake. It may want to observe with being thankful for your family, your home, your health, and your life.

Another step in the direction of crafting a positive personality is to begin any venture or challenge to get to learn and gain knowledge from it. Keep in mind, whether or not you reach your goals or your intention, and whether you attain it or not, the process will add knowledge and experience to your life and makes it more enjoyable. If you begin a challenge or task to analyze from it, you will by no means be disappointed. That is the way you broaden wisdom.

Determine the area that needs to be changed. If you want to be more optimistic and think more positively, first identify areas of your life that you usually think negatively about, such as your work, daily commute, or relationships.

Focus on one area to tackle it more aggressively. Check yourself and stop from time to time throughout the day and evaluate your thoughts. If you find that your thoughts are mostly negative, try to find a way to make them have a positive meaning. ...Keep it humorous. Let yourself smile or laugh, especially in difficult times. Have a sense of humor in daily activities. If you can laugh at life, then you will feel less stressed. You can also subdivide the whole day into 10 minutes on weekdays.